FUN FACTS AND HABITATS: BELUGAS

Imaginative adventures, fascinating facts, and hands-on activities about Belugas through the eyes of Bella the Beluga.

ELLIE BLOOM

TABLE OF CONTENTS

GOOD NIGHT, OCEAN
BELLA'S GOODBYE
THANK YOU FOR LEARNING WITH BELLA THE BELUGA WHALE!

HELLO, I'M BELLA!

Hi there! My name is Bella, and I'm a beluga whale. I live in the chilly Arctic waters and love to sing, swim, and play with my pod. My white color makes me look like I'm always smiling. Let's go on an adventure to learn all about me!

Fun Fact:
Beluga whales are called "canaries of the sea" because they are so vocal

SNOWY WHITE

Unlike other whales, I’m all white! This helps me blend in with the icy snow and water around me. When I was born, I was gray, but I turned white as I grew up.

Fun Fact:
Belugas turn white as they become adults—baby belugas are gray!

MY MELON HEAD

I have a soft, round bump on my forehead called a melon. It helps me make sounds and find my way around underwater. I can even move it around!

Fun Fact:
The melon helps belugas use echolocation, like a built-in sonar!

SINGING WHALE

I love to sing! I chirp, whistle, and click to talk to my friends. That's why people call me the canary of the sea.

Fun Fact:
Belugas can make over 50 different sounds!

FRIENDLY FAMILY

I live in a pod with other beluga whales. We travel together, hunt together, and protect each other. We're a big happy family!

Fun Fact:
Beluga whales live in pods of 2 to 25 whales, but sometimes even hundreds!

ICE, ICE, EVERYWHERE

I live in cold places where the water can freeze into ice. I can swim under the ice and even find breathing holes to pop up for air!

Fun Fact:
Belugas can break thin ice with their backs to breathe!

WHERE I LIVE

My home is in the Arctic Ocean, near places like Canada, Russia, and Alaska. Sometimes I travel to rivers too!

Fun Fact:
Beluga whales are one of the few whale species that can swim in both salt and fresh water!

NO DORSAL FIN

Unlike dolphins or orcas, I don’t have a dorsal fin on my back. This helps me swim under icy waters without hurting myself.

Fun Fact:
No dorsal fin helps belugas glide easily under the ice!

MY NECK MOVES

I can move my head side to side and up and down. That's because I have loose neck bones just like you!

Fun Fact:
Belugas have seven neck bones, just like humans, and theirs are not fused!

ARCTIC SWIMMER

I love swimming through chilly Arctic waters! My thick blubber keeps me warm, even when the ocean is super cold. I glide through icy waves like it's nothing at all.

Fun Fact:
Belugas have a thick layer of blubber that can be up to 5 inches thick!

FISH FEAST

Mmm, dinner time! I love to eat fish like salmon and herring. I slurp them up with my small teeth and never chew—just gulp and go!

Fun Fact:
Belugas eat over 50 different types of sea creatures!

CHATTERBOX

When I'm with my pod, we never stop chatting! We whistle, chirp, and click all day. It's how we stay close and have fun.

Fun Fact:
Belugas can even mimic sounds they hear, like a human voice!

PLAYTIME FUN

I like to play with bubbles and chase fish for fun. Sometimes I even play with seaweed like it's a toy.

Fun Fact:
Belugas are very playful and love to interact with objects in the water!

TOOTHY GRIN

I have about 34 teeth, but I don't use them to chew. I grab my food and swallow it whole, just like that!

Fun Fact:
Belugas use their teeth to catch and hold food, not to chew it!

SMILING FACE

People say I look like I'm always smiling. My curved mouth and bright eyes make me look happy—and I am!

Fun Fact:
Belugas are one of the only whales that can change their facial expressions!

ECHO MAGIC

I use echolocation to see in dark water. I make clicking sounds, and they bounce off objects, helping me find my way!

Fun Fact:
Belugas can tell the size and shape of objects just by listening to echoes!

BABY BELUGAS

When beluga babies are born, they're gray and swim close to their moms. They drink milk and learn how to swim and sing.

Fun Fact:
Beluga calves stay with their mothers for up to two years!

RIVER VISITS

Sometimes I swim into rivers during the summer. The water is warmer, and it's a great place to find food.

Fun Fact:
Belugas can travel hundreds of miles upriver!

SNOWY SONGS

When the snow falls, I keep singing under the ice. My sounds bounce all around, and I love to hear them echo!

Fun Fact:
Sound travels better in cold water, making beluga songs extra powerful!

WRINKLY SKIN

In summer, I shed my old skin by rubbing on rocks and sand. It feels good and keeps my skin healthy.

Fun Fact:
Belugas are one of the only whales that shed their skin!

LONG TRAVELER

I love to travel! My pod swims far across the ocean to find food and safe places to rest.

Fun Fact:
Some belugas travel over 3,000 miles each year!

WHALEY SMART

I'm a smart whale! I solve problems, remember places, and work together with my pod to find food.

Fun Fact:
Belugas have one of the largest brains of any whale!

BODY ROLL

Sometimes I roll around in shallow water and rub my belly on the ocean floor. It's how I stretch and clean myself.

Fun Fact:
Belugas love to roll and twist in shallow water!

SUMMER FESTIVAL

In the summer, hundreds of belugas gather in river mouths. We splash, play, sing, and have so much fun!

Fun Fact:
Beluga whales gather in large groups during summer to molt and socialize!

WHITE AND BRIGHT

My white color helps me stay hidden from predators in snowy waters. It's perfect for the Arctic!

Fun Fact:
Belugas are the only all-white whale species in the world!

TAIL POWER

I use my strong tail to swim fast and dive deep. With one big swoosh, I'm off like a rocket!

Fun Fact:
Belugas can swim up to 14 miles per hour!

BALLOON HEAD

My melon isn't just for looks. It helps me send out sounds and understand the world around me.

Fun Fact:
Belugas can change the shape of their melon to focus sounds!

OCEAN EXPLORER

I explore icy oceans, deep seas, and river bends. There's always something new to discover!

Fun Fact:
Belugas are found in the Arctic and sub-Arctic waters around the world!

SAFE TOGETHER

We belugas take care of each other. We swim in groups, help each other, and stay close.

Fun Fact:
Beluga pods work together to protect calves and find food!

BUBBLE RINGS

Sometimes I blow bubbles just for fun. I make rings and chase them—it's like playing tag!

Fun Fact:
Belugas can blow bubble rings from their blowholes!

A WHALE'S TOUCH

I like to gently rub against my podmates and nudge them. We use touch to stay close and show love.

Fun Fact:
Belugas use their bodies to communicate affection and playfulness!

GOOD NIGHT, OCEAN

At night, I rest while still swimming slowly. My brain stays half awake so I can watch for danger.

Fun Fact:
Belugas sleep with one half of their brain awake to stay alert!

BELLA'S GOODBYE

Thanks for swimming with me, friend! I had so much fun telling you about my life. Remember, the ocean is full of wonders, and I'm always out here, splashing, playing, and living free!

Fun Fact:
Belugas are one of the most curious and playful whales in the sea!

THANK YOU FOR LEARNING WITH BELLA THE BELUGA WHALE!

Printed in Dunstable, United Kingdom

64562105R00047